Pebble® Plus

LET'S LOOK AT COUNTRIES

LET'S LOOK AT
SOMALIA

BY A. M. REYNOLDS

raintree

a Capstone company — publishers for children

Raintree is an imprint of Capstone Global Library Limited, a company incorporated in England and Wales having its registered office at 264 Banbury Road, Oxford, OX2 7DY – Registered company number: 6695582

www.raintree.co.uk
myorders@raintree.co.uk

Edited by Erika L Shores
Designed by Juliette Peters
Picture research by Jo Miller
Production by Kathy McColley
Originated by Capstone Global Library Ltd
Printed and bound in India

ISBN 978 1 4747 6945 7
23 22 21 20 19
10 9 8 7 6 5 4 3 2 1

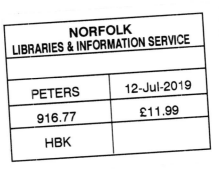

British Library Cataloguing in Publication Data
A full catalogue record for this book is available from the British Library.

Acknowledgements
We would like to thank the following for permission to reproduce photographs:
Alamy: Angela Fitch, 8; Dreamstime: Patrick Wangari, Cover Bottom; iStockphoto: muendo, 9; Newscom: Reuters/ Feisal Omar, 1, 15, Cover Top, Reuters/Omar Faruk, 13, Reuters/STR, 12, robertharding/Liba Taylor, 16, 17, Universal Images Group/De Agostini/A. Tessore, 3; Shutterstock: Afonso Martins, Cover Middle, Cover Back, Free Wind 2014, 19, 22-23, 24, Globe Turner, 22 (Inset), HelloRF Zcool, 6, Homo Cosmicos, 20, imeduard, 21, nate, 4; Wikimedia: AMISOM Photo / Ilyas Ahmed, 5, AU-UNIST Photo / Stuart Price, 11.

Every effort has been made to contact copyright holders of material reproduced in this book. Any omissions will be rectified in subsequent printings if notice is given to the publisher.

All the internet addresses (URLs) given in this book were valid at the time of going to press. However, due to the dynamic nature of the internet, some addresses may have changed, or sites may have changed or ceased to exist since publication. While the author and publisher regret any inconvenience this may cause readers, no responsibility for any such changes can be accepted by either the author or the publisher.

CONTENTS

Where is Somalia?

Somalia is a country in Africa. It is nearly three times bigger than the UK. The capital city is Mogadishu.

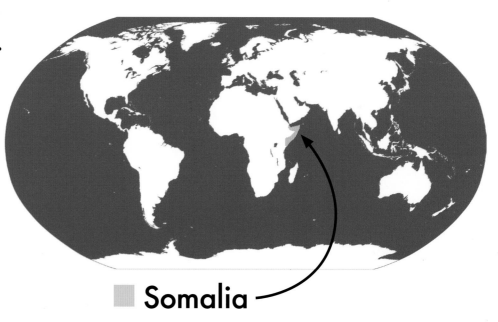

Somalia

Mogadishu, Somalia

From deserts to mountains

Much of Somalia is flat desert.

There are mountains in

the north. The climate is hot.

Somalia does not get much rain.

In the wild

Some big animals live in Somalia.

Lions hunt in the grasslands.

Camels walk across deserts.

Hippopotamuses lie in the rivers.

lions

camels

9

People

People in Somalia speak both Somali and Arabic. Families often have more than five children. Most people in Somalia live in small villages.

At the table

Milk is a popular drink.
Somalis drink cow, camel and
goat's milk. People living by
the sea eat fish. For breakfast, Somalis
often eat pancakes called anjero.

anjero

Festivals

Everybody is invited to weddings.

People dance and sing. In July,

Somalis celebrate summer.

They build bonfires, splash

water on each other and dance.

At work

Many Somalis look after camels and cattle. Others catch fish or work on large banana or sugar cane farms. In cities, some Somalis work in factories.

bananas

Transport

In the countryside, people ride

camels and donkeys to get to places.

Only a few roads are paved.

People travel on buses for longer trips.

In the city, some people drive cars.

Famous place

Laas Geel is a group of caves in northeastern Somalia. There are rock paintings of people and animals inside the caves. These paintings are more than 5,000 years old.

QUICK SOMALIA FACTS

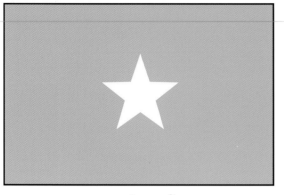

Somalian flag

Name: Federal Republic of Somalia

Capital: Mogadishu

Other major cities: Hargeysa, Berbera, Kismaayo

Population: 11,031,386 (2017 estimate)

Size: 637,657 sq km (246,201 square miles)

Language: Somali and Arabic

Money: Somali shilling

GLOSSARY

capital city or town in a country where the government is based

celebrate do something fun on a special day

climate usual weather that occurs in a place

bonfire big outside fire

hippopotamus large African animal with thick skin and wide jaws; hippos eat plants and swim in water

FIND OUT MORE

BOOKS

The Amazing Continent of Africa (Engage Literacy), Jay Dale (Raintree, 2017)

Children's Illustrated Atlas (DK Children's Atlas), Andrew Brooks (DK Children, 2016)

Introducing Africa (Introducing Continents), Chris Oxlade (Raintree, 2014)

WEBSITES

www.dkfindout.com/uk/animals-and-nature/hippopotamuses
Find out more about hippopotamuses.

www.dkfindout.com/uk/earth/continents/africa
Find out more about Africa.

COMPREHENSION QUESTIONS

1. Why do the Somalis who live by the sea eat a lot of fish?

2. What is the capital of Somalia?

3. What is inside the caves at Laas Geel?

INDEX